Potty Train
In Three Days

Potty Train In Three Days

Lois Kleint, M.A., Ed.

Jean Kleint, Editor

Creating Gifted Kids Enterprises
San Diego, California

www.creatinggiftedkids.com

Published by
Creating Gifted Kids Enterprises
San Diego, CA
Fifth Printing: © 2013 Lois Kleint
Fourth Printing: © 2011 Lois Kleint
Third Printing: © 2007 Lois Kleint
Second Printing: © 2005 Lois Kleint
First Printing: © 2002 Lois Kleint

ISBN 0-9716399-0-6

Ann Huisman
Cover, Book Design, Photography & Prepress
ahadesigner@cox.net

Jasen Haskins
Photography
intuitivedesign.com

Printed in the United States of America

For additional copies of this book contact:
lois@creatinggiftedkids.com
www.creatinggiftedkids.com
www.facebook.com/pages/creatinggiftedkids/62960454398

This book is dedicated to
all the little toddlers who attended my schools.

You taught me much over the years.

Contents at a Glance

Introduction

Yes, you CAN potty train your little one–confidently, pleasantly, and permanently—in only three days.

This book provides the easy step-by-step procedures. If followed consistently, they will enable you and your child to experience successful potty training without frustration or failure.

Over the years, I have discovered and tested many principles and techniques to guide and train toddlers and young children into desirable, positive behaviors, not only for potty training, but for numerous other stages of childhood. It has been my privilege over a 30-year career to have a great deal of opportunity to study young children and develop these new and unique methods for training toddlers and youngsters.

My life's work as an educator has encompassed the wonderful roles of teacher and school principal, preschool director and early childhood specialist, child-rearing educator and parenting counselor. These roles have been inter-woven with my delightful experiences as a mother of four and grandmother of ten.

After training and consulting with parents for a number of years, those familiar with my ideas began to urge me to share these methods with a greater audience. Thus, I offer to parents everywhere these principles and techniques, knowing that you will have success if these guidelines are carefully followed. As these principles are incorporated into a daily relationship with your child, there will be effective results not only in potty training, but in many other areas of your child's life.

These methods are based on principles of behavior that are as dependable as the laws of gravity. We have personally potty trained hundreds of children in my nursery schools using this three-day program, and have counseled hundreds of parents on how to potty train their own children successfully at home.

I encourage you to read through this book completely to familiarize yourself with the specific techniques before beginning potty training.

Above all, I encourage you to have fun with your toddler while you are potty training. Your attitude means every-thing when guiding your child into this new behavior. May it be an enjoyable and successful experience for you and your child alike.

Lois Kleint, M.A., Ed. — San Diego, California

Prepare Yourself First 1

You will first need to prepare yourself before attempting to train your child for potty training. Toddlers cue their behavior not only from your words and actions, but also from your unspoken signals and mental attitudes. Therefore, in this chapter you will prepare yourself mentally, by learning a new way to think about potty training.

Described below are several potty-training "myths" which parents have erroneously believed to be true. As you read them, along with the facts presented, you will be able to free yourself from any of these misconceptions. Also described in this chapter are the signs of physical readiness that you as a parent will need to look for in your child, as well as guidelines for choosing the proper timing for potty training.

Once you have prepared yourself by learning how to think about potty training, how to identify the signs of physical readiness, and how to chose the right timing, you will then be ready to go on to the step-by-step procedures detailed in Chapters 2 and 3.

1. *Free Yourself of Potty Training Myths*	Parents are hesitant to begin potty training for a variety of reasons. In most parents' minds, it is a monumental task to undertake, one which they would rather leave to happenstance or chance. Parents' fears and objections can be dispelled by the knowledge of simple truths. The truth is that you can and should train your child to have success in this stage of his development.

Fact:
It is a fact that by the age of two (and certainly by two-and-a-half), a child's body has developed enough for him to consciously control his bladder and bowel.

Certain traits of physical readiness are observable at this age. Many children are ready by 18 months or earlier; most all are ready by age two, and certainly all children can be potty trained by 30 months. Exceptions are children challenged by severe physical or learning disabilities.

Myth #2:
"I don't want to potty train my child at age two. He is still a baby, and I want to enjoy his babyhood; potty training will make him grow up too fast."

Fact:
To keep a toddler in the baby stage when he is showing readiness for the next step can actually hinder his social and psychological development.

Parents need to be keenly alert to a toddler's rapid, daily changes and keep up with their child's growth. The goal is *to avoid* protracting the child's state of immaturity. If he is encouraged as a toddler to progress from stage to stage, within the appropriate windows of opportunity, he will grow up to be a more capable person in every way. In this formative stage the child sets lifelong patterns of behavior, from which will stem much of his future capacity for maturity, successful relationships and personal growth. It is important for parents to be aware of progressive stages in toddlerhood, including the all-important stage of potty training, and to recognize when your child is ready for this step. *Help your toddler to attempt new things,* rather than holding him back.

When a toddler masters one behavior, this will empower him to progress toward the mastery of other developmental behaviors. Without conquering early stages of toddlerhood, a child's further development can be thwarted. Potty training is a key stage in your child's life, for which he needs to experience success before he can progress to other sequential stages of his development.

Some parents feel that a baby's early years are merely for their personal enjoyment, so they attempt to keep their child in an infant state. The wise parent, however, will recognize that this type of parental behavior can set a pattern for dependency in later life. By continuing to change his diapers when your child shows readiness for the potty, you make him feel incapable of doing things for himself. You are conveying the unspoken message, "You are still a baby. You are not able to use the potty. You need diapers. You cannot do things for yourself." The truth is that you can enjoy each progressive stage of your child's life, and help him to develop and mature in a timely way.

Myth #3:
"My child may suffer psychological harm if I initiate potty training. He should tell me when he is ready, or even teach himself."

Fact:
There are actually developmental benefits for the child when the parent initiates timely potty training.

I have often encountered parents who fear they will psychologically damage their young child if they initiate potty training. A common question is, "Can't I wait until my child uses the potty on his own?" This idea may stem from the counsel of well-meaning friends and relatives or "experts" unfamiliar with the successful and proven methods suggested here. However, my experience has shown the opposite to be true: more psychological harm can be done by parents who leave the young child to his own devices, than by parents who guide and train their child, and give him much-needed firm and loving direction.

Although it is necessary to look for signs of physical readiness, a two-year-old is not mature enough to decide *when* it is time for toilet training, or to train himself. In his short lifetime, he has had little experience in decision-making. That is a skill which must be taught, and one which will develop as he grows and matures. Meanwhile, at the toddler stage, you must take the responsibility to make his decisions for him. Give him firm direction, and then allow him to work at a task and attempt to do it for himself. However, it should be at your initiative and direction that he takes action. With a two-year-old, you need to assume that he does not know what he really needs. Help him by being very *specific* in your instruction and assistance. This produces *security* in a youngster. Later on, give him progressive opportunities for decision-making. At age two, he needs guidance in order to be led into positive ways.

A child will find security in a parent's loving direction with simple, positive commands and consistent follow-through. This basic principle will guide parents in teaching any behavior to young children.

Nature teaches that parental urging is needed. A mother eagle does not wait for her baby birds to decide to fly. Instead, she trains them and pushes them out of the nest at the proper time. This is true of many creatures for their various stages of physical development. It is also true for our children's development.

Myth #4:

*"I believe that my
child is not ready for
training, because he
balks at using
the potty."*

Fact:
**Balking is not an indication
of a lack of readiness; rather, it
is a typical two-year-old reaction
to any request.**

Most children are excited about using the potty, if training time is approached with parental enthusiasm. However, some children may occasionally protest going to the potty by saying "No," or displaying other negative behavior. This is often an automatic response from two-year-olds on many issues, including potty training. Such behavior quickly disappears when the parent makes a decision, and confidently, methodically and patiently carries through with it, guiding the child step by step. Success comes as parents respond with decisiveness and consistency. Ignore the negativity and require positive behavior by not backing off. The wise parent will not allow a child to balk; he is not swayed by protests, and does not allow himself to be backed off or to be directed by a two-year-old.

Fact:
Less time is required in the long run if parents plan ahead and give a few days of concentrated focus to potty training.

Far from being an easy task, raising a child requires an all-out effort to do it well. It is more convenient to take the easy way out. However, some parents actually stand in the way of a child's development for the sake of their own convenience. Potty training is one stage that parents avoid for various reasons, such as upcoming events or busy work schedules. Disposable diapers have also provided an easy way to keep children in this stage. Parents may rationalize their inaction by thinking that their child will eventually learn to use the toilet on his own. However, letting your child stay in diapers long past his second birthday makes training much more difficult for you, the parent. Believe me, real inconvenience comes when trying to train the older child and having to deal with problems caused by having pampered your own desire for "convenience." Potty train when your child shows readiness, and don't put it off!

2. Look for the Signs

Now that we have eliminated some misconceptions, the next step is to study your child, and decide when he is ready.

Begin looking for signs of physical readiness for potty training between the ages of 18 to 24 months (sooner with some children) so you can catch him at the opportune time. Children tend to go through cycles of readiness and unreadiness within a few weeks. Training is easier when your child *first* shows even a few of the following signs:

1. **Waking dry after a nap or a night's sleep.**

2. **Trying to take off a wet or soiled diaper.**

3. **Wanting to wear underwear instead of diapers.**

4. **Wanting to sit on the toilet.**

5. **Showing interest in watching others who have mastered the function.**

6. **Showing awareness that he is about to soil his diapers.**

7. **Informing you after the fact that his diaper is wet or soiled.**

3.
Make Your Decision

Once you see that your child is ready, the next question is: Are *you* ready to take on the challenge of potty training, and give it the concentrated time required? Most people think timing is up to the child. **However, once he is showing physical signs of readiness, success is determined much more by your decision and attitude than by your child's.** If you are doubtful, your child will intuitively sense your feelings and have a more difficult time mastering this new behavior. It is important that you feel confident about the timing for potty training.

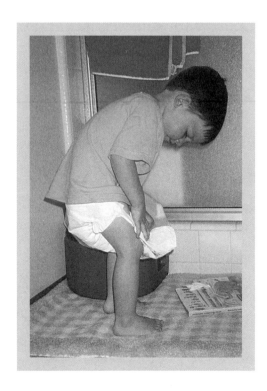

Here is an example of the importance of timing. One of my two-and-a-half-year-old nursery school students was showing signs of wanting to be potty trained. The parents were not supportive of the idea but agreed to allow the nanny to train the child while they were out of town. The mother cringed at the thought of the child peeing on her new white carpet, and the father did not want "his baby" to grow up. On the other hand, the nanny realized that the child was ready. The child was successfully trained by the nanny during the parents' three-day absence.

When the parents returned to a child who was potty trained, they voiced doubt instead of expressing faith in the child's ability. The mother told the nanny, "Sure, she goes potty for you, but she won't do it for me." The father actually expressed disappointment that the nanny had potty-trained his daughter. As a result of these parental attitudes, the little girl was unable to maintain her new behavior. Within a few days she regressed, and the mother began to diaper her toddler again.

This story shows how important it is for the parents, as well as the child, to be ready. A child needs encouragement and nurturing to be successful in any new behavior. Cues come from the parent, so without support the child can become discouraged, and actually regress.

Every adult involved in the child's life must support the potty-training process. Parents, of course, are the most influential forces in a child's life, with the nanny, teacher, and baby-sitter as secondary influences. Ideally, therefore, parents should be the ones who begin the training process. Then other supportive adults can take over and maintain that training. You will want to ensure that your child's other care providers also read this book, so they can support the child and follow through with the procedures you initiate.

4.
Set The Time | Find the best time for you to devote your focus to this training. There can be a myriad of reasons for beginning. There are factors that can guide you as you set your timetable. Many parents begin when expecting a new baby, when Mom is expecting to return to work, or when the child will enter preschool where potty training is required. Regardless of the circumstances influencing your decision, once you begin, don't waver until the process is completed.

Make plans so you can give the training your entire attention for a few days. This is an important key for success. Arrange for time off from work and plan to alter your daily routine. The training will need to be the focus of your entire day for the initial three days. Be willing to give up your work, errands, and baby-sitters. Find a good time to take a three-day weekend when you can be home. This will create a positive time for your child to make him feel special and loved. Select a time when you and your child are physically and emotionally in good health. Timing is best when there is a minimum of tension in the home and outside pressures are minimal. For example, do not attempt to train your child when he is teething, weaning, or has any illness. Examples of other undesirable times may include when the child is upset by Daddy being out of town, when Mom has just started a new job, when the family has just moved into a new home, etc.

Once you have prepared yourself mentally, made your decision, and planned a time for potty training, you will then need to prepare your child for the "Big Day" — his first day of potty training...

Prepare Your Child 2

reparing your child ahead of time for the **Big Day** consists of several steps. In this chapter we will discuss such issues as weaning your child, playing potty, obtaining the necessary equipment and clothing, and verbally talking to your child about the training period several days before you begin it.

You will want to involve your child in each of these steps throughout the preparation process. **Eliminate any sudden "surprises" and talk him through each step ahead of time, so he knows what to expect.** This is an important principle in any type of training or new experience for your child. He will feel secure (1) if he knows what to expect and when, and (2) if you carry through with what you tell him you will do. It can be detrimental to a child to suddenly surprise him by informing him of things at the moment an event takes place, or allowing him to experience something without any prior preparation or discussion on how to think about it. Even when the unexpected occurs beyond your control, you can talk your child through it and teach him how to think about it. In this same way, you can help your child to feel confident and secure during the potty training process by talking it through and preparing him ahead of time. Follow the simple steps of preparation that are listed below.

1.
Provide
Examples
from Birth

As every parent knows, young children learn from what they see in their family environment. It is important for a baby to be raised in an atmosphere where he can observe family members in the functions of elimination. This will help him to have a much easier time of potty training, because the procedures will already be within his experience. Allow your baby occasions to be in the bathroom with siblings or parents. Then when he is a toddler and it is time for him to be trained, he will feel more comfortable about the pottying process.

2.
Wean | Before attempting potty training, gradually wean your child from the bottle, breast, and pacifier. Bottle and breast feeding cause excess liquids and greater difficulty in bladder control, thus less success in potty training. Also, bottle, pacifier, and breast dependency give the unspoken message that your child is still a baby. Potty training, on the other hand, signals leaving the baby stages behind, and this new behavior should ideally follow after complete weaning has been accomplished.

For the final stages of weaning from bottle and pacifier, parents should follow a procedure similar to the "Diaper Tossing Ritual" discussed later in this book.

3.
Create Interest | Another helpful way to prepare your toddler is to read him stories about potty training ahead of time. You may also want to show him videos on this subject. You can find a number of interesting books and videos designed for toddlers in your library or bookstore.

4.
Play Potty

As previously mentioned, one sign that your child is ready for training is his interest in sitting on the toilet to "play potty." This role-playing stage should be encouraged to give him a feel for "potty" before he actually begins training on the Big Day. At the "play potty" stage, you may also want to try putting your child on the potty when he wakes up dry from a nap or night's sleep. However, do not pressure him or expect success during this play period; just let him have fun and develop confidence.

5.
Prepare with Simple Equipment

Some of the basic items needed to help create the potty training environment are a potty chair, a toilet ring, and a step stool. You will want to prepare for the training period by obtaining these items ahead of time. Include your child when shopping for or obtaining this equipment, and talk with him about it. Because of its short-term use, you may want to borrow this equipment from other parents rather than purchasing it.

Potty Chair — Potty training is much easier if, to begin with, your child uses a small potty chair with a bowl underneath. This will allow parents to monitor when the child has actually urinated. The chair will only be needed for the first week or so, or until the child is comfortable with the idea of toileting. A good unit to buy is the type of potty chair that sits on the floor, but which can also be converted to a simple ring for the regular toilet. Some also come with a step stool.

Toilet Ring — After a week or so of successfully using the little potty, you can graduate your child to a toilet ring, which is used on top of the family toilet seat. This will help your child feel safe and secure while on the big potty. Normally, after a few days, the use of this ring can also be discontinued.

Step Stool — A small step stool should also be available to allow the child to eventually get up onto the family toilet himself. The stool can also be used to reach the sink so the child can wash his hands.

6.
Prepare with Appropriate Clothing

Underwear – Plan to take your child shopping for new underpants before the Big Day. Purchase underwear decorated with your child's favorite cartoon or other special characters. Talk about the underwear and use lots of affirmative comments, such as these:

"We are buying this new, special underwear for potty training day."

"Soon you will wear underpants, and not diapers."

"You will learn to pee and poop in the potty, not in your diapers any more."

"You will keep your new underwear nice and dry all day long."

Clothing — During training time, dress your child in simple, loose clothing. Soft shorts or pants with loose elastic waists will enable him to pull his own clothes up and down. This will make him feel like he can do it himself, and will ease him into the "big boy" stage.

7.
Purchase Rewards

Prepare ahead of time before the training begins by having a few simple rewards on hand. These little surprises as rewards for his successes could be such things as a small toy, a little treat, sticker, etc.

8.
Begin Talking to Your Toddler a Few Days Before the Training

The next step is to talk to him ahead of time, letting him know what will be happening. Begin this verbal preparation only three or four days before the actual potty training period, conversing with him about the actual day when he will begin to regularly use the potty. This verbal preparation is very important, and you will sense when it has accomplished its purpose. The process of repetition will reach his young mind as you tell him over and over all day long:

"You are getting bigger like Mommy and Daddy."

"Diapers are for babies. You are going to go potty like Mom [or Daddy]."

"You have new, special underwear and you are going to keep them dry all day long."

"No more diapers. We are going to throw the diapers away. You will not need them any more."

"You will love to go potty."

"Mommy and Daddy will be so proud of you."

Praise the child continually to build his confidence. Let him know that this will be a good thing for him: help him feel that you are rooting for his success; you are going to help him and be with him when he learns to pee on his little potty seat. Tell him he will not need diapers, and that he can be big like his parents and siblings, etc.

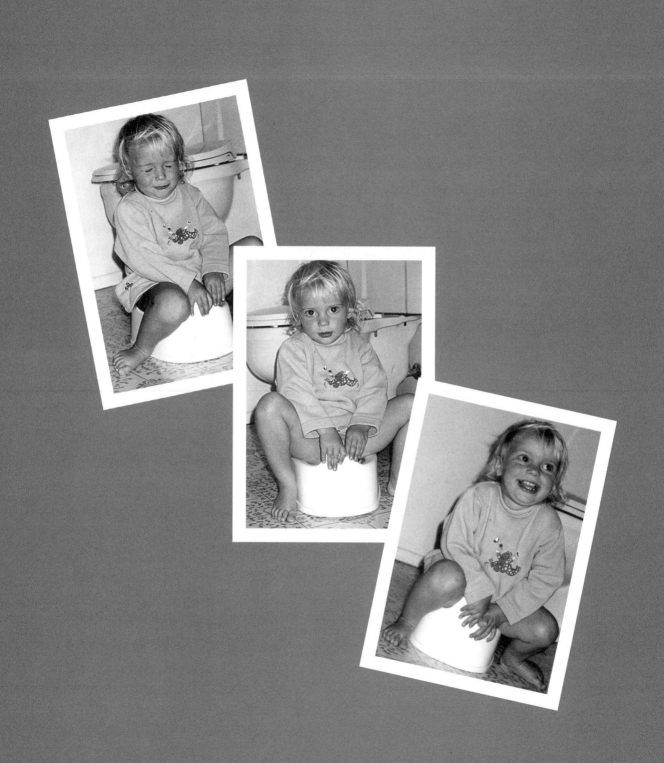

Follow Step-by-Step Procedures 3

Day One

The "Big Day" has arrived. You are prepared, your child is prepared, and the time has been set aside to concentrate on potty training. This is a special time for your child, a day when all your other obligations are laid aside, and you can give your time to training and loving your little one.

Ideally, only one person should be initiating the training during this first day, and preferably the same person for all three days. If you are unable to be with your child during the entire time, carefully instruct his other caregiver so that he or she will be supportive and follow through with your procedures.

Keep in mind that this training needs to be precise and ordered at your direction. The steps described below are based on specific, proven principles of learning, and need to be followed carefully. **The goal for this first day is learning to sit on the potty at your direction, rather than looking for results.**

1. *Celebrate the Diaper Tossing Ritual*	Use this procedure on the first day of training. Before your child is even dressed for the day, begin talking to him about no longer needing diapers, and about how the two of you will throw them away together. Talk him through this using very simple statements, such as:

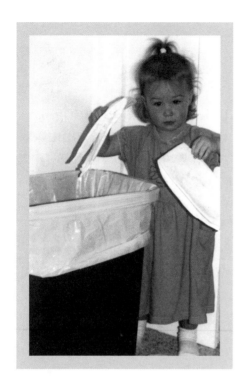

"No more diapers!"

"We are throwing away the diapers because you are big now."

"You will use the potty and wear underpants."

"Throw the diapers away."

"We do not need diapers anymore! You will pee and poop in the potty."

Then, toss the diapers together.

It may be of help in describing this procedure to share one mother's story of the "diaper tossing ritual." She tells about how she waited until the day of the weekly trash pick-up to start the first day of potty training. That morning, she helped her child drag the last bag of disposable diapers outside to the large outdoor trash can, and throw them in. Then mother and toddler together pulled the trash can to the curb. A little later, the child heard the garbage truck rumbling up the street. She ran to get Mommy, and the two watched while the family's trash can was emptied into the truck. As the truck disappeared down the street, the child was wide-eyed, and stated contemplatively, "No more diapers!" By walking through that experience with Mommy, the child had internalized that she would have to use the potty from then on.

You can make this a joyful and fun event for your child, talking about how he now gets to use the potty; he will be more grown up, because he will not need baby diapers any more. Whether you rid the household of diapers by actually throwing them away or giving them away, **the important thing is that your child senses a finality about not using diapers anymore, from now on**. Don't purchase any more diapers, or even "pull-up" disposable underwear. Then you can begin your first day of training.

2.
Get Your Child Dressed | Next, after getting rid of the diapers, it is time to help your child dress for the Big Day. Lay out your child's underpants and loose clothing. Make a special presentation of them, and make it a fun occasion. If his final diaper from the previous night is wet, make no mention of it.

Show him how to put on his new underwear as you help. Speak to him with enthusiasm and encouragement:

"I want you to keep your new underpants dry all day long."

"You are so big now, you are going to pee in the potty."

Rather than saying, "You cannot pee in your new underpants," the emphasis should be on statements of positive encouragement. **Tell him what he can do, rather than what he cannot do.** This is an important principle in training a child. Positive remarks give him a goal and direction.

3.

Use the Potty Every Hour

Next, after dressing, announce with enthusiasm that it is time to go potty. Then, hold your child's hand and take him to the bathroom to use the new potty chair. You will need to visit the bathroom every hour that the child is awake. Monitor his nap times so that when he awakens you can take him immediately to the potty. Wake him if he naps too long.

Your focus for this first day will not be so much on the child successfully eliminating on the potty, but on learning the procedure of pottying. Do not express any disappointment to the child.

The simple behavior of going to the bathroom and sitting on the potty at frequent intervals will, in itself, eventually set a successful pattern.

Regardless of what is in the potty at the end of each session, you are simply getting him familiar with using the potty. That is your first day's goal.

Between the hourly potty visits, watch for the telltale signs that he may be about to go.

Take the attitude, "I'm not going to let him experience the defeat of peeing or pooping in his pants; I want to help him be successful."

Because you will be with the child every moment, you will learn the signs that indicate when he is about to go in his pants. Watch for facial expressions, tensing, and overt actions such as hiding. These indications signal that he needs to use the potty.

Catch him *before* the fact, and hurry him to the bathroom (carry him if necessary, at first). Then have him sit on the potty-chair. Encourage him. In this way, the potential negative experience can be turned into a success, before he has a chance to go in his pants.

Until the skill of successful pottying is repeated for a couple of days, do not allow your child to play at the potty between your directed time intervals. The "play potty" period is over for now. Unless he really needs to go, steer him away from the bathroom until it is time for the hourly ritual. It is important, during this time period, that potty time be at your direction. You may want to close the bathroom door when it is not in use.

4. *Make Potty Use a Required Activity*	During training, do not ask the child if he wants to get on the potty. Instead, simply say to the child, "It is time to go to the potty." Then take his little hand and lead him to the bathroom. He needs specific direction through manual guidance and very simple verbal commands. **Avoid explanations and excess discussion while training.** This is a very important key.

During the training, direct the child as to when he should get on and off the potty. The child should not make his own decision about when to sit down or jump up off the potty.

Do not ask the child what he wants to do. To give a toddler choices can cause confusion and insecurity, and you will not accomplish the desired goal. Firm yet loving direction will make him feel secure. Tell him what to do and when.

5.	Teach the child how to pull his clothing up and down
Teach the Child to Pull Down His Own Clothing	if he is not already able to do so. Take his hand in yours, helping him to learn by doing. Help him to insert his thumbs on both sides of his clothing at the waist and assist him in getting his pants down. Then place his thumbs around back so he can pull down the clothing below his bottom. Learning this step is a part of training.

As with any new learning situation, the first time, you may do it for him; the next time or two, do it with him, showing him "how," step by step; then finally, let him practice doing it himself, while you monitor his progress. If, however, the parent continues to pull the child's clothing up and down for him, this will soon rob the child of an important learning experience. Do not keep your child dependent on you in this way. Even though it is easier and less time-consuming for you to do things for the child, let him do it for himself after he knows how. This is important for the child. It helps him to feel like a confident little person.

6.

Stay With the Child

During training, while the child is on the potty, **do not leave his side.** At this point, he should stay on the potty at least three minutes, but no longer than five minutes for each visit. While he is sitting on the potty, make him feel it is a special and positive time by singing or reading to him, or talking about interesting things. Tell him how big he is and how fun it will be to keep his new underpants dry all day. Let this be an unhurried, cheerful time for both of you, a time of experiencing the excitement of learning something new.

Remember to repeat these procedures every hour, on the hour, for the first day or so.

7.

Train Little Boys Properly

At first, and until the child becomes adept at using the potty, have your boy sit down on the small potty just as you would a girl. This will make it as simple as possibly for him when first beginning potty training. This is especially important because peeing and pooping may not be recognized as separate functions at first.

First, help him pull his pants all the way down to his feet. This will keep his clothing dry in case he misses. Once seated, teach him to push his penis down to point at the bottom of the potty; pull his knees together for him to keep his penis pointed downward. Tell him, "Hit the bottom with your pee." After a very few times, he will know the procedure, if you start him out in this manner. Once you feel he is competent at this (after a few days to a week), you can graduate him to the toilet ring on the family potty. You will teach him to sit on the large toilet in the same way. When he is adept, then you can teach him to stand up at the big potty, telling him to pee in the water like Daddy or big brother. This may require a short step stool to elevate the child to the necessary height.

Some little boys are ready right away to stand. If your child indicates an interest or displays readiness, do not discourage him. The goal is to keep the child progressing from one level of learning to the next.

8. *Take the Child Off the Potty*	As indicated earlier, your child should get off only at your direction. He should not be allowed to jump off and on the potty. He needs to know this is a time for training, not play. After he has been sitting for a few minutes, take his hand and tell him, "Now it is time to get off the potty."

9. *Look Into the Potty*	After you take the child off the potty-chair, together look to see if there is any pee. If there is none, simply say, "No pee yet. Maybe next time," and praise him. If he does pee in the potty, celebrate successes as indicated in point 13. Then

have the child himself empty the little potty bowl into the family toilet.

10. *Practice Wiping, Flushing, and Hand Washing*	Make these rituals part of potty training, whether the child pees or not. Hold the child's hand as you pull off the toilet paper and teach him how to wipe. When he graduates to the big potty, or after he has successes on the potty-chair and dumps them into the big potty, then practice flushing. Help him overcome any fear by letting him watch as the toilet paper disappears with the pee and the water. After

pulling up clothing, teach him to close the lid. Then help him up on the step stool and teach him to wash and dry his own hands. There is more to pottying than peeing in the toilet. Teach your toddler good bathroom hygiene as well.

You will need to continue to monitor potty behavior for a few weeks, avoiding toilet paper games such as unrolling a whole roll or over-stuffing the toilet. Show him exactly how much to use, a small enough amount for a little hand, and do not allow him to play with the paper.

Diligence in teaching these procedures from the beginning shows the child what **to** do. When the positive behavior is taught from the beginning, it becomes the child's experience; he does not know any other behavior in this situation, because it has not been allowed. **The principle here is to direct the very young child's actions.** Rather than leaving him to his own devices, and later needing to "untrain" him from bad habits developed on his own, it is best to never allow the undesirable behavior in the first place. This ounce of prevention is worth a lifetime of cure.

11. Be Patient While Your Child Masters Bowel Movements

Proficiency with bowel movements sometimes comes later. This can become discouraging both to the child and the parent unless you help him develop a pattern. You need to be attuned to your child, especially if he is not regular in his bowel movements. Little boys, especially, may not associate "pooping" with the "peeing" process. You may know his pattern, or be able to sense when it is time. Because you are with him constantly at first, you can usually catch him in the process of a bowel movement. You may see your child stop his activity, tighten up his face and frown, or make a grunting noise. Take him to the potty immediately, even if you need to carry him. Do not give him any sense of alarm, but move quickly. If you can catch him three times successively, he will get a feel for pooping in the potty. Then praise him and help him wipe. The same process of course applies to little girls.

12.
Work Through Any Fear or Resistance | Very few parents using this method ever encounter resistance. A child prepared with excitement and enthusiasm for this special time in his life will not usually balk at potty training. However, some children will protest the first few times they are put on the potty, voicing a "no" response, or some other protest. If your child balks when presented with this new procedure, you may need to repeat the preparation stage.

If you sense his hesitation is fear, especially when graduating to the family toilet, walk him through it with gentleness, helping him to understand there is no reason to be afraid. Let him watch family members use the toilet. Encourage him to push the flush mechanism. Tell him that you won't let him fall in. Show that you are not afraid. Hold him continually while he is on the toilet. You may need to return him to pottying on the small potty seat for a while.

A key principle with any area of training is to ease your child into doing what he fears in order to get rid of that fear.

Do not leave your child to suffer for months or years with a particular fear. You can walk him out of any unfounded fear at an early age. Help him; be with him; encourage him. Walk him through it, talk him through it, and he will see that there is nothing to fear.

For potty training fears, talk to him gently all the while, hold him while he sits on the potty, and tell him that you will not let him get hurt. Stand close to him and let him feel your support. Guide his hands, hold him, and encourage him, to make him feel secure. With your confidence, the child will learn, in no time, that there is nothing to fear. Most importantly, deal with the fear, and don't back off; leaving him to live in fear can harm him psychologically. In addition, you will delay the training process, and miss the window of opportunity at this optimal stage.

13.
Celebrate His First Success

The first time your child pees or poops in the little potty seat, you should have a celebration. Do this

in your own way to show your excitement. Clap your hands, sing songs, jump up and down, or dance around the room. Encourage and praise him with great enthusiasm. Wipe up and clean up, and then give him one of the little rewards that you planned for him. You may also want to call Daddy on the phone. Whatever you choose to do, celebrate in some way. Love him,

hug him, talk to him, praise him.

Your enthusiasm, however shown, will do more to encourage further successes than anything else in the training process.

The praise and reward you give for positive behavior is a much stronger force for change than any punishment for negative behavior. Children want and need your approval. Be sure to show it.

Once a child has had several successes, he will have developed the positive behavior of going in the potty, which replaces the negative behavior of peeing in his clothing. You are actually breaking an old pattern by creating a new one. This takes a great deal of effort and repetition for a few days, but the pay-off is well worth it.

Rewards should be discontinued after one or two days. **However, continue with praise.** After a few successes, if the child has an accident before you can catch him, his clothing should be immediately changed. Help him as needed. Later, if he continues to have accidents, you will use the procedures described in Chapter Four.

If you are willing to give this much attention and effort to this process, you will have a dry child in a few days. Both of you will be happier for it. An intense focus is required to give your attention to the child every minute, for a couple of days, but your diligence will pay off. Hundreds of parents can attest to the success of these procedures, when followed carefully.

14.
Make Naptime and Nighttime Consistent With the New Behavior

Before naptime and nighttime, for these three days, give your child as little liquid as possible. Fortify the child's mattress with extra padding. Put the child on the potty immediately before sleep. **Do not use diapers or pull-up style disposable training pants, at night or during nap-time.** Use extra heavy cloth training pants. Plan to wash sheets and mattress pads for the first night or two if needed. Your child will be trained within three days if you stick with it. Let him know you believe in him and trust him, and he will ultimately wake up dry. One mother fortified her child's bed with a towel decorated with favorite cartoon characters. The child loved the towel so much that he did not want to get it wet. This was a good motivation for the child to avoid wetting the bed.

Day Two

Once these procedures have been followed for Day One, you may find that your child is nearly trained by the end of the day. Continue, however, on the second day, following the same routine as Day One, modifying as needed. Again, give potty training your total priority and guard your time with your child. The reward of eliminating all other responsibilities during this time is that you will never have to deal with toilet training again. By the second day, you will become attuned to your child's toileting pattern. You may find that he needs to be taken to the potty every two hours, or every half-hour. Modify the timing of this training procedure to fit your child's own personal pattern. Later on you will take him less frequently.

In the morning, when your child first stirs to awaken, whisk him to the potty. Do this before he has time to fully wake or wet his bed. You may need to carry the child to the potty the first morning or two to help him have a success after waking.

For naptime, take your child to the potty before he lies down. When he awakens, follow the same procedures for morning waking.

Day Three

Proceed to methodically take your child to the potty at regular intervals, as in the previous two days. By now, he will most likely be well on his way to proficiency in toileting. Then you can begin to modify procedures, as discussed in Chapter Four.

Practice Makes Perfect 4

Your child's new behavior will be established within this initial first three days. However, for the next few weeks, he will continue to need parental reinforcement. How long it will be needed depends upon the child. This is as important as the initial potty training.

For at least a few more days, keep taking the child to the toilet at regular intervals, as before, with praise for every success. Remain consistent and vigilant. At this point, you can begin to enlist the help of other family members and care providers. Be sure they follow your same procedures to avoid confusion for the child. Modify frequency and timing as needed.

During the **first three days** the child **learns** the behavior. Within the **first three weeks** he **practices** it, and becomes adept enough for you to depend on the consistency of his behavior. In most cases, he will be completely trained in three days, but will require follow through.

Graduate your child to the regular toilet some time within the first three weeks of the training process. This will help the child to feel more like the rest of the family. Use the same bathroom during this two- to three-week follow-up period, until the child is comfortable with toileting.

Here are some basic guidelines for this three-week follow-up period, after initial training.

1.

Modify Procedures

After he begins to master his new skill, you will no longer need to assist with such activities as limiting liquids, helping with clothing, giving instructions, requiring him to use the potty every hour, or having him sit on the toilet for five minutes. Be sensitive to your child to determine when you can gradually back off from each of these steps.

2.

Allow Potty Practice

After a few successes, the child may again want to "play potty." Immediately after children have learned to pee in the potty, some may want to do it every few minutes. If your child wants to play potty at this point, he is simply practicing his new skill. Once the initial training period is over and he is experiencing success, patiently go along with him during this stage while he practices and enjoys his newfound success. This phase will pass in a day or two.

3.

Handle Accidents With Care

After you feel that your child has mastered toilet training (normally within the first two to three weeks), it is not uncommon for him to revert back to old habits and begin to have accidents. At that point, you should express some disappointment about accidents. Don't say, "That's all right," because it is not all right, and you should not confuse the child by making him think that it is acceptable when he knows it is not. However, you need to be kind and not express anger or disgust. Simply tell him that accidents are no longer acceptable. Tell him, *"You need to keep your underwear dry. You are a big boy now. You can pee and poop in the potty."*

Then require the child to change his wet or soiled clothes if he has had an accident. You may have to assist somewhat, but let your child experience the unpleasantness of changing soiled clothing. Tell him, matter-of-factly, to take off his wet or dirty underpants. Then let him work at it on his own; don't do it for him. When he has put on dry clothing, tell him to put the wet (or dirty) clothes in the laundry area. Let him carry the clothes from the bathroom. Usually two or three episodes will help him realize he has control and can avoid this situation; the associated unpleasant consequences will motivate him to stay dry.

For little boys, once they learn to stand at the toilet, this process should include cleaning up the floor for peeing "misses." Don't do this for him; have him wipe up the floor himself, using a mild cleaning product and paper towels to get the floor clean. You will be surprised at how quickly this procedure will help him learn to aim properly. A clean floor for years to come will make you glad you took the time to pay attention and follow through in this detail of the pottying process.

4.
Graduate to the Big Toilet

Once your child has successes and no longer needs the little potty seat, he can graduate to the toilet ring on the family toilet, or to the family toilet itself. The toilet ring may be used as long as it is actually needed. There is no hurry to graduate from the ring to the large toilet seat. However, even very young children can learn to use the family toilet with proficiency. In fact, some children may not need to use the ring at all.

To use the family toilet (with or without the ring), the child should first pull up a stool and stand up on it in front of the toilet. Then ask him to turn around and pull his underwear and pants down to his feet. It is important that you hold him so he feels secure. Help the child (boy or girl) to sit down carefully on the front edge of the potty, showing him how to brace himself with his hands by holding on to both sides of the toilet seat. Verbally and physically assure him that he is safe. Stay at his side every minute, holding him as long as necessary. After two or three times with help, he will be comfortable enough to do it on his own.

After little boys feel comfortable with sitting on the big toilet, you can teach them to pee standing. Some may need to stand on the stool.

5. *Remind* *Your Child* *of Potty* *Time*	**For as much time as a month or two, you will need to assume the responsibility of reminding your child to go to the potty and wash his hands, as he may not yet be able to assume the responsibility on his own.**

Continue to remind your child to go on a fairly regular schedule. You may need to go with him. Some two-year-olds may need to be supervised every moment; others can simply report back to Mommy after toileting.

Small children can pee on command. When you know it is about time, simply say, "It is time to go potty!" Then have the child sit long enough to get even a few drips in the potty before allowing him to jump down and go elsewhere. This way, he will stay dry until the next

scheduled attempt. (Obviously, this will not be required every hour.)

Often a discouraged mom who has just potty-trained will say to me, "My child does not tell me when he needs to go potty." I explain that for most two-year-olds, it is difficult for their little minds to compute that they must head for the bathroom when they need to, or to even realize their need to pee or poop. **In these first stages, they must be told regularly when it is time to go. Part of the learning process is for the child to become aware. Learning to know ahead of time, to sense when it is time to go, is a key element in your child's potty-training success**. Your insistence on regular potty visits will establish the healthy habit of developing his elimination awareness, and contribute to the self-esteem needed to reinforce pottying success.

If you faithfully follow the steps outlined above, within three weeks, your child will have thoroughly mastered potty training. He will feel a sense of accomplishment at this successful stage in his young life. Your reward will be the beaming smile on his young face. Congratulate yourself, too! You did it! Be sure to give yourself a reward for a job well done!

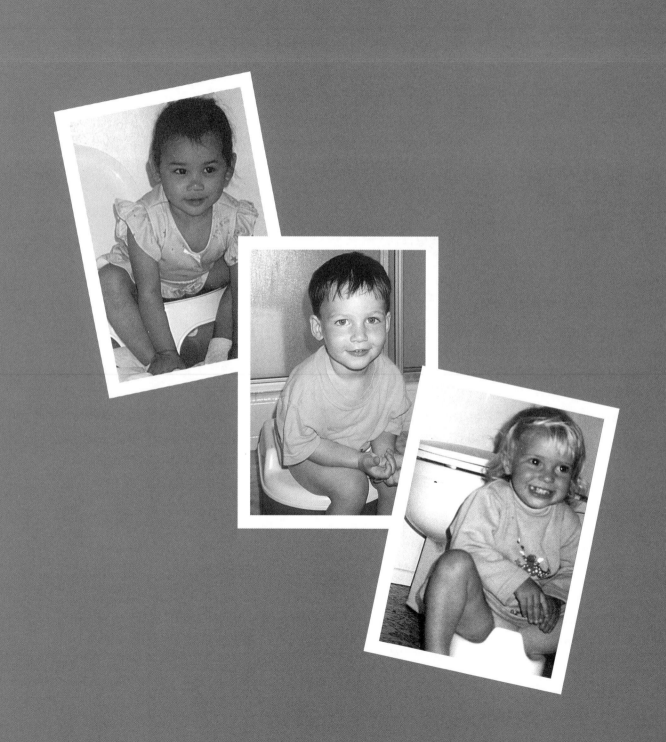

You may have a few additional questions before attempting potty training, or wonder what to do about issues that come up during the training period. Here are some commonly asked questions that concern parents, along with some simple solutions.

1. Question: "What if my child does not respond to these procedures? After weeks, nothing seems to work. Day after day, it is as if he had no training."

Answer: If you have difficulty training your child, examine two possible reasons for the lack of success:

a. The child's environment - First take into account the timing and the atmosphere for training. Forces at work in the child's life at the time may be the hindrance. Is the child or the parent ill? Is the child concerned about Daddy being away from home? Is child or parent experiencing a time of emotional difficulty? Consider the timing and conditions of your attempted training period and attempt again later on, before examining the next possible factor.

b. A possible learning disorder - After many years of successfully training hundreds of small children, I have discovered that a child with a learning disability such as Attention Deficit Disorder (ADD) or Attention Deficit Hyperactivity Disorder (ADHD) will usually have difficulty with potty training. An ADD or ADHD child will not only have trouble learning to use the potty, but he will also be untrainable in other areas of his life. He may exhibit traits of noncompliance, inattention, impulsiveness, mood swings, hyperactivity, etc. (You may wish to read the informative material about ADD/ADHD located on the website *about.com*.) Because of this dysfunction, such a child has trouble learning from consequences, as do normal children. Unpleasant consequences such as soiled clothing may not register with him. This disorder may actually cause distractions that prevent him from sensing his bodily functions. Therefore, maintaining awareness and control over his body can be more difficult for him than for other children.

You may already have sensed by his second birthday that your child has such a disability, although doctors often postpone diagnosis until a child is of school age. It has been identified in children as early as two years of age. The potty-training inability may be one of your first indications of a learning disorder. However, do not use this as an excuse to avoid potty training for any child. Even this child will learn, but usually much later than normal children.

For this type of child, patiently work at it until you see success. You cannot leave this child to his own devices. Even more than other children, he needs parental guidance and high levels of structure in his life. Be aware that potty training will require your constant attention for a much longer period of time than it would for other children, but do not avoid training.

A few children without learning disorders are simply willfully noncompliant. This is often due to parents' failure to require cooperation in any other area of his life. However, if you really begin to work at motivating them, these children **can** control their behavior. By contrast, the ADD/ADHD child is **unable** to comply or to control his behavior.

2. *Question: "What can I do about a two-and-a-half-year-old who learned to pee in the potty very quickly and easily, but holds his bowel movements for long periods and then goes in his clothing?"*

Answer: In such cases, the child may not have made the connection between peeing and bowel movements. Parents often have to train for two separate functions. Talk to him and help the child to understand that he must also poop in the potty. Watch him carefully for the signs mentioned previously. At the moment you catch him, simply tell him he needs to go poop in the potty, and take him quickly to the bathroom. One success will help to give him the idea. Catch him three times in a row, and he will have it figured out forever. For parents this means "being on duty" vigilantly for a period of time. Avoid reactions of anger with such a child.

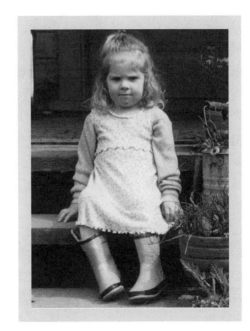

3. *Question: "What can I do about an obstinate toddler who will pee and poop in his pants anywhere?"*

Answer: Here, consistency is the key. I often find that such a parent is not consistently attending to the child during every waking hour of the initial three days of training. If the problem occurs later on during the first few weeks, it may be because the parent fails to continue taking the responsibility to get the child to the potty at regular intervals.

As discussed, the parent or caregiver needs to be on duty at all times for a few days in order to make the potty training period effective. All day long, this person needs to be alert to the child's behavior. Your goal is to intervene **before** wrong behavior occurs, and take him to the potty immediately when you sense he is about to pee or poop. Even spending a moment or two away from the child can set him up for failure. For instance, if Mom takes a shower when the child is awake, she needs to first give the child to another responsible adult to monitor his pottying needs. Because the child is not able to train himself, someone must be available literally every moment of the day during training. This cannot be stressed enough. Parents must consider themselves on duty during this time. That is why I recommend an initial concentrated training period of three days, so the child will learn a solid foundation of pottying behavior. This he will do in a few short days, if he has your full attention and if you are consistent.

To remedy this situation later on, do what you would do if you were just beginning potty training; begin all over again, following the guidelines outlined in this book, and maintaining the needed vigilance. You and your child will have success in no time.

If you are persistent in requiring a new behavior such as pottying, and the child senses that you will not become discouraged and back off, he will comply with your wishes and continue in the new behavior. However, a hit-and-miss approach confuses the child, and he will do whatever he pleases at the moment, instead of wandering over to the potty on his own. Instead of **expecting** him to do so on his own, at this point, it is the parent's responsibility to **require** him to do so, and to take him regularly. Even after the initial training period, regular parental follow-through is needed. **It is actually parental inconsistency that causes the misbehavior. Correct the child in this situation by correcting the parental inconsistency.**

4. Question: "How can I help my child stay dry during sleep? He always wakes wet, and I feel that I need to go back to diapering him at night."

Answer: **Please, do not go back to diapering.** This confuses the child and gives him "permission" to pee at night. There are several things you can do instead to help this child. This subject warrants additional attention, and the additional discussion below.

Decide that bed-wetting is unacceptable to you. It must become important to you that your child stops wetting during sleep. Realize this is not necessary or acceptable behavior. **Decide** that this is going to change, and do not sympathize or make excuses for the child. One mother told me that her child wet the bed until he was twelve years old. "My other child will probably do the same," she said. To believe such things, or to speak this in the child's hearing, merely reinforces negative behavior, and gives both of you an excuse to avoid proper potty training.

You need to be assured that this situation is easily corrected when you follow these procedures. Children respond positively when parents make a decision, and stick to it firmly with follow-through.

***Focus on the positive*. Tell the child what he is going to do, rather than what he should not do**. Your focus needs to be on creating new behavior, rather than on discouraging the wrong behavior. Talk to the child enthusiastically, positively and frequently throughout the day (even hourly), by saying simply:

"You are going to stay dry while you sleep."

"When you wake up, you are going to pee in the potty."

"You are so proud of your new underpants; you want to keep them dry."

"You really want to keep your bed and your new blanket dry."

Help your child have success by helping him feel that you are supporting him. This is an important key. Few children will be successful in a new behavior without parental help, so make your child sense that you are there to help him succeed. Be supportive. Do not react. Avoid anger, harsh commands, disapproval or disappointment in your voice tones. Talk him through the idea that he is going to stay dry. A child also learns by the words he speaks with his own mouth, so help the child to speak the same affirmations you speak to him. Help him to feel confident.

Monitor liquids carefully. Start cutting liquids to only a small amount (half a cup), during the two or three hours prior to going to bed. Then, one-hour prior, try letting him go without any liquid. Just before sleep, allow him only a small sip or two of water. This can be modified once he has learned to stay dry, but at first he needs this strict procedure to experience success.

Wake the child during sleep. For a few days, wake him during sleep to go potty. Try to be aware of when he pees. For some, it is shortly after they go to sleep; for others, it may be early morning. Notice when your child wakes at night; this may be right after he wets his clothing. Try waking him just before this time the next night, and help him go quickly to the potty while he is still sleepy. Wake him a bit early in the morning and carry him or take him to the potty while he is waking. Be patient, and not critical. If your child is a heavy sleeper, you may need to do this for a period of time.

One parent slept on the floor near the child for three days, and caught the child stirring every morning about 5:00 a.m.; she quickly took the child to the potty each time, and successfully had him nighttime trained in three days. She felt that it was well worth the loss of sleep for a few days to train her child in this way; the child soon began to wake, walk to the potty himself early each morning, and then return to bed! The secret of the mom's success was that she could be nearby to learn the child's nighttime habits, and train him accordingly. She did not give up, but determined to help him have success, whatever it took to do so.

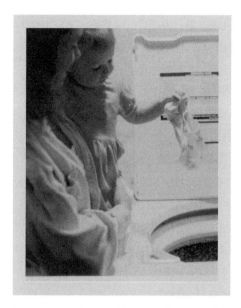

Give your child an incentive. To help him to stay dry during sleep, tell him there will be a special prize for him if he wakes dry. If he wakes wet, of course, do not give him the prize. Give him encouragement and offer the prize to him the next day if he stays dry. This pleasant thought in his memory before bed can help motivate him to stir himself and get to the potty in the early morning when the urge strikes, instead of falling back to sleep and peeing in his bed.

Require the child to change his clothing. Always. Even in the middle of the night. Don't do it for him. Do not give him an excuse for wetting by providing a change of clothing that has been set out nearby. That gives him a mixed message. He may feel that you are expecting him to wet his clothes.

By way of example, I share the story of one mother who always brought extra clothing to nursery school for her little girl in case she peed at naptime. Although this child was potty-trained, the mother **expected** her to wet during nap, **believed** that she would, and sent extra clothes to school; therefore, the child always **did** wet at naptime! One day the mother announced to the teacher, "Oh, I forgot to bring a change of clothes!" The little girl overheard and, consequently, she did not pee in her clothes during naptime that day. She knew she had no recourse but to stay dry. The next day, when the mother again brought a change of clothing, of course, the child wet her pants during naptime! Be aware that a child will do what you expect him to do, positive or negative! **Parental expectation is a powerful force.**

Be Consistent. Do not diaper your child some days and put underpants on him other days. Do not use nighttime pull-up style disposable underwear. If you are inconsistent, your child will also be inconsistent in his pottying behavior. In order for you to be consistent, go back to the guidelines on parental preparation. Plan ahead. Be sure that you lay aside everything else you are doing for initial training. Remember that this requires your focus for only three days or three short weeks out of your lifetime, but it will be worth everything to your child.

Be patient and loving. Don't give up. Re-read these guidelines, and add any steps you may have omitted. Consider this to be a challenge that can and will be met with success!

(Note: If after attempting all of the above, you still have no success, you may want to seek a doctor's medical opinion. However, it is very rare that a medical condition prevents pottying success. Normally, these procedures, if carefully followed, will resolve the problem).

5. *Question: "How can I train my two-year-old when his four-year-old brother still wears disposable underwear, and wets and poops his pants nightly?"*

Answer: Normally, there is only one way to accomplish this: you will need to address the older brother's toileting problems before you introduce your younger child to potty training.

6. *Question: "How can I successfully train an older child? My son is four years old and not yet potty trained."*

Answer: If you have a three-year-old or a four-year-old child who is not yet potty trained, you may be wondering if it will ever happen. You may be frustrated, discouraged, embarrassed, or even feel disgust. However, don't give up hope. Specific procedures and extra effort will bring successful potty training for the older child. Realize, however, that you will encounter more resistance to your efforts at this age.

By age three, children settle into behavior patterns that become difficult to reverse. An untrained three- or four-year-old may be medically normal, have no hyperactive problems, but simply be accustomed to using diapers, because parents have allowed it. However, by re-training with the methods in this book, his behavior can be redirected. He can and will learn to use the potty.

In such a situation, **your attitude** is the major factor. You will need to regain a positive attitude by clearing your mind of the memories of frustrating past failures, and, with a new attitude, begin again. Realize that the situation is neither good nor bad; it is just a fact. Say aloud to yourself frequently, "I will not be judgmental or frustrated. My child can be potty trained, and I will have faith in his ability." Rehearse these words aloud to yourself until this thinking is internalized. Small children are more sensitive to attitudes than to words, so you will need to believe it in order to help your child believe in himself. You can be confident, knowing that a child of this age is physically able to master pottying.

Several days before again initiating a training period, tell the child wonderful things about himself and how he is going to behave. Use affirmations similar to those listed earlier. In this way, the older child will feel support and sense your confidence in his ability. Children are impressionable and believe everything you tell them. Take advantage of this trust. **Also, be aware that children overhear more than you know. Be positive—and be careful—about what you voice in conversation to others about your child.**

Then, follow the same procedure that you would use for the younger child. The day you begin training lay out his new clothes and announce to him, "This is the day you are going to stay dry. You are going to be a big boy and use the potty from now on." Continue with the steps listed previously, remembering to praise your child, thus giving him confidence. Consistent re-training with careful attention to procedures, and insisting that the child use the potty instead of diapers, are the keys here.

7. *Question:* "*What should I do if my potty-trained child suddenly reverts to peeing in his pants after several weeks of success?*"

Answer: As discussed earlier, there may be times when he pees in his pants after you think he is adept at his newly learned behavior. This is not uncommon; in fact almost all children will slip back, once or twice. At this point, treat it as though this is not acceptable behavior, but do so **without** punishment. Think of it as an isolated incident, and do not make an issue out of it. He will be back on course in a short time.

The most successful method in this situation is to have the child clean up his own mess, take off his own clothes, and put them in the wash area. Then, afterwards you can lay out fresh clothing for him to put on by himself. If he realizes Mommy will not clean up his mess, and that he will have to struggle to get his clothes off and on, he will gain a new perspective on his behavior. A bath may also be required. Sometimes it may be helpful to matter-of-factly require the child clean up the bathroom floor or toilet for messes caused by waiting too long to go to the potty. This is particularly true for the older child, who may simply be ignoring bodily signals for too long while continuing to play. If he realizes he will have to clean up messes and clothing, it will not be worth it to him to delay when the consequences take so much more time than the desired self-control would take. For younger children in this situation, you may find for some that just talking to them and encouraging them to stay dry is enough. However, in some other cases, I have recommended that the parent again give the child rewards for staying dry for a day or two. This usually gets them back on track.

These answers should cover most of the questions you may encounter. In summary, the best solution is to read and re-read: keep reading this book during the preparation, training, and follow-up periods, until you feel you know the preciseness, the order, and the positive attitude that will make this work for your child. Then, expect success!

Conclusion

This book represents a positive approach to training children. However, it requires parents to place definite demands on the child; the commands and expectations are not optional. The child needs to be guided and directed in each step. Parents sometimes think this means that they must be harsh, unkind, or mean to the child in order to give him commands or be in control. Nothing could be further from the truth. You can be kind, yet specific in your demands, requiring specific behavior from your child.

> **Remember that:**
> - **Consistency breeds security.**
> - **Once you get started, don't back off.**
> - **Parents are in control, not kids.**

Using the procedures in this book, I have had success with over 95% of all the children and parents I have worked with for over 15 years. However, there have been a few parents who have not been successful with these methods. These were: (1) Parents who lacked a positive relationship with their child and were already unable to maintain any kind of control in other areas requiring discipline or consistency in their child's life; and (2) parents whose children had a learning disability, which may have caused the parents to give up on training. On the other hand, countless numbers of children have been quickly and easily potty-trained by following these simple procedures.

You, too, can potty train in three days. Three seems to be the magic number in working with little children. In three tries, three days, three weeks, any new behavior can be established. By repetition, children's behavior patterns are set quickly and internalized in their thinking and habits. It is this factor that causes these methods to have a high rate of success.

Teaching an important life skill such as this to your child will more than reward both of you in the years to come. These same procedures, walking him through each step and staying with him until you are sure he can follow through on his own, can be used for many areas of his life to create a well-behaved child. You will thank yourself for sticking with it during the early years when you see the results in a loving, respectful, orderly young adult. You'll be glad you paid attention to the details of careful nurturing during toddlerhood with a positive attitude toward your little one. Your child deserves all the effort you can give!

Please remember that, above all, you need to think of parenting as an adventure. Have fun with your child. Be loving and consistent. When all is said and done, and your child has successfully attained potty skills, be proud of your accomplishment and his—and celebrate success for both of you!

My sister goes potty.

Tayler-Ann Haskins, Age 8